Cool STEAM Careers

ROBOTICS ENGINEER

WIL MARA

Published in the United States of America by Cherry Lake Publishing
Ann Arbor, Michigan
www.cherrylakepublishing.com

Content Adviser: Nick DePalma
Reading Adviser: Marla Conn, ReadAbility, Inc.

Photo Credits: ©Joe Bibby, NASA Robonaut/http://www.flickr.com/CC-BY-2.0, cover, 1, 9; ©Roger Dale Pleis/Shutterstock Images, 5; ©carroteater/Shutterstock Images, 6; ©Tyler Olson/Shutterstock Images, 11; ©Corepics VOF/Shutterstock Images, 13; ©NASA Robonaut/http://www.flickr.com/CC-BY-2.0, 14; ©U.S. Customs and Border Protection/http://www.flickr.com/CC-BY-2.0, 17; ©Monkey Business Images/Shutterstock Images, 19; ©Stocktrek Images/Thinkstock, 21; ©ndoeljindoel/Shutterstock Images, 23; ©Matc13/Thinkstock, 24; ©Steve Jurvetson/http://www.flickr.com/CC-BY-2.0, 27; ©Official U.S. Navy Page/http://www.flickr.com/CC-BY-2.0, 28

Library of Congress Cataloging-in-Publication Data

Mara, Wil, author.
Robotics engineer / Wil Mara.
    pages cm. — (Cool STEAM careers)
  Summary: "Readers will learn what it takes to succeed as a robotics engineer. The book also explains the necessary educational steps, useful character traits, and daily job tasks related to this career, in the framework of the STEAM (Science, Technology, Engineering, Art, and Math) movement. Photos, a glossary, and additional resources are included."— Provided by publisher.
  Audience: Ages 8-12.
  Audience: Grades 4 to 6.
  Includes index.
  ISBN 978-1-63362-006-3 (hardcover) — ISBN 978-1-63362-045-2 (pbk.) — ISBN 978-1-63362-084-1 (pdf) — ISBN 978-1-63362-123-7 (ebook) 1. Robotics—Vocational guidance—Juvenile literature. 2. Systems engineering—Vocational guidance—Juvenile literature. 3. Vocational guidance—Juvenile literature. I. Title.

TJ211.2.M37 2015
629.8'92023—dc23   2014031659

Cherry Lake Publishing would like to acknowledge the work of
The Partnership for 21st Century Skills. Please visit www.p21.org
for more information.

Printed in the United States of America
Corporate Graphics

ABOUT THE AUTHOR

Wil Mara is an award-winning and best-selling author of more than 150 books, many of which are educational titles for young readers. Further information about his work can be found at www.wilmara.com.

TABLE OF CONTENTS

STEAM is the acronym for Science, Technology, Engineering, Arts, and Mathematics. In this book, you will read about how each of these study areas is connected to a career in robotics engineering.

The Future Is Now

Michael was watching a documentary on television. It was about a musician who had lost his hand in an accident but was able to relearn piano after he was fitted with a **prosthesis**.

"That's amazing," he said to his older brother. "It's like his whole arm has turned into a robot."

"Kind of," his brother said. "My friend at college is studying how to design those. He wants to be a robotics engineer."

When you hear the word *robot*, you probably think of

things like science fiction movies and aliens in spaceships. You might imagine metal machines that look kind of like people and talk in funny, computerized voices. The simplest definition of a robot is a device that can make changes to the world around us. That is not a new idea.

A prosthesis is designed to work like the body part it replaces.

This ancient water clock is an example of a robotic machine.

Countless cultures have myths and legends that include machines. Ancient Greeks told of a living bronze statue named Talos who protected the city of Crete. In Christian folklore, the German bishop Albert the Great is said to have built an **android** out of solid brass to act as a servant and adviser.

There are numerous mentions of actual robotic machines found in ancient texts. These machines were known as **automatons**, and they performed relatively simple tasks with very little human interaction. One of the most famous was a water clock dating from around 250 BCE. It measured the passage of time through the steady flow of water.

The great artist Leonardo da Vinci was interested in robots. Toward the end of the 15th century, he built a mechanical knight using a suit of armor and a series of gears and pulleys. The knight could sit down, stand up, raise the visor on its helmet, and move its arms around.

THINK ABOUT ENGINEERING

An engineer is a person who gathers scientific and mathematical information and then uses it to create something of practical value. You have to not only come up with the idea of a robot, but also create the robot.

Today, robots are no longer just part of human imagination. They're here, and they're here to stay. There are robot cars, robot waiters, robot teachers, and robot animals. There are robotic prostheses for people who have lost limbs, and some of them are incredibly realistic. There are robots that mow lawns, vacuum carpets, and clean swimming pools.

There are also robots called surrogates that look so much like real people—everything from facial expressions to voices—that it's nearly impossible to tell the difference. And that's just what's happening *now*. Who knows what we'll see in the years ahead? Are you interested in taking on one of the biggest challenges of the 21st century?

The National Aeronautics and Space Administration's
Robonaut was built to help humans work and explore in space.

GETTING THE JOB

Robotics engineers are the ones who design and build robots. A robot operator will then use the robot during daily work. Math and science skills are required to become a robotics engineer, but so are creativity and inventiveness. Not everyone has these talents, but those who do will find themselves in high demand.

Education is the first step, and this can be a little tricky. Hardly any colleges offer a degree in robotics engineering. You'll have to approach this career a slightly different way—by getting a different engineering degree. The most

Robotics engineers are usually people who like to invent things.

helpful engineering degrees for robotics are usually electronics, mechanical, or software. With one of these, you will gain the knowledge you'll need. You can expect lots of classes in science, mathematics, and computer hardware and software. Other useful classes may include robotics manufacturing, computer-aided design (CAD), programmable logic controllers, mechanical systems, **hydraulics**, and **microprocessing**.

A four-year degree, known as a bachelor's, is the minimum requirement to get into robotics engineering. A high school diploma is not enough education. But you greatly increase your chances of getting a job with a master's degree or a doctorate.

Following your college graduation, you may need to pass certification exams. These vary from state to state, but they deal with the same subject matter. The Fundamentals of Engineering exam should be taken immediately after you get your degree.

Robotics engineers benefit from classes in hydraulics.

Working as an intern with an experienced robotics engineer provides a student valuable experience.

14

Once you've completed your education, passed your exams, and been hired for an entry-level position, you will likely receive further training. This training may be done on the job, which will give you valuable hands-on experience. You'll want to get all the experience you can in the early stages of your career. You might be able to work as an **intern** or as an **apprentice**. Just remember—a robotics engineer has the potential to earn very good money, but this will probably not be the case during the first few years.

THINK ABOUT TECHNOLOGY

To keep ahead of your competition in any field, a broad knowledge of the most current technologies will benefit you. This is particularly important in a career like robotics engineering, where improvements in all aspects of the field are happening all the time. The person who keeps up on the latest developments will be the one most in demand by employers.

DOING THE JOB

If you enjoy mathematics and science and are a creative thinker, then robotics engineering could be a dream job for you. Robotics is being used more often and in more situations, so you also would have the thrill of working in an area that is at the forefront of modern technology.

The daily work of a robotics engineer has two main elements—designing robots and then overseeing their production until a working model is completed. The first part, design, considers the robot's purpose. Other factors to consider are the robot's working environment, the cost limitations, how much human interaction will be needed, and whether the robot's appearance will be important. So the first step is gathering as much data as possible concerning the robot's requirements.

Some robots are designed and built to work underwater.

From there, the engineer begins the design work. This stage happens mostly on a computer screen, although some engineers still like to make their rough sketches on paper and later move them to computers.

Fortunately, the average robotics engineer has not only excellent design software but also excellent **simulation software**. This demonstrates how a robot will perform under various conditions before you go to the time, trouble, and expense of actually building it. "Sim" software cannot, of course, foresee *all* circumstances, but it can get pretty close.

Once the robot's design has been determined, the engineer will supervise the production of the **prototype**. The materials used must be durable and functional. The engineer will also be involved in the careful programming of the robot's software, as this will be the machine's "brain." The software is what receives the commands from the engineer and then translates them into the robot's eventual actions.

A robotics engineer designs the robot and supervises the building of a prototype.

After a robot has been built, the testing phase begins. A robot will be put through numerous tests and pushed beyond its required limit in order to assure that it will be able to handle any situation. The testing phase is when the engineer works outside of an office or laboratory. For example, a robot designed to roll along the hot and rocky surface of Mars should be tested in a desert environment. Many robotics engineers find the testing phase to be the most difficult, because problems always occur. But eventually seeing your creation finally work is very rewarding.

THINK ABOUT ART

A robotics scientist uses creativity combined with math and science skills to come up with never-before-tried ideas. Make-up artists, special-effects artists, puppeteers, and latex designers also add artistic elements to robots. The finished robot may seem like only a machine to other people, but it is artwork in the truest sense of the word.

Robots like this K10 Rover are tested on Earth before going into space.

Good Days, Bad Days

Like any other profession, robotics engineering has its ups and downs. While most days are fun and challenging, others can be tense, stressful, and frustrating.

Robotics engineering isn't generally dangerous in the same way as being a firefighter or a police officer, but it has its share of hazards. You will sometimes be working with extremely powerful equipment, and since you are the person who designs and tests that equipment, you should expect the unexpected.

The construction of a new robot can also be very stressful. It requires an enormous investment of time, energy, and manpower. Someone is financing the project, and that person will be looking for results. Since you will be undertaking a process of invention, mistakes

Care must be taken when working with powerful robotics equipment.

Watching a successful test of something you've designed and engineered is extremely rewarding.

are to be expected—but only to a point. As the engineer, you are supposed to take an idea and turn it into reality. Some people thrive on that kind of pressure, but not everyone does.

On the positive side, a robotics engineer gets to work both with a group and individually. A robotics engineer may spend much of the design phase working alone, in an office with sketches and a computer nearby. When it comes time to build the robot, the engineer will lead other people in the building process. Later, during the testing phase, the engineer often not only designs the tests but gets to watch them take place.

A robotics engineering profession comes with many rewards. Generally, a robotics engineer will earn a very good starting salary and has the potential to earn even more money with more experience. There is also the enormous satisfaction of knowing that your creations might contribute to a better world in areas such as medicine, manufacturing, teaching, and public safety.

THINK ABOUT MATH

Every mathematical computation has to be precise. How much pressure should be applied by the robot when it goes to pick something up? How fast will it need to travel? How much battery energy will it use before it has to pause and recharge? Each calculation is critical, and each aspect of the robot's design will be determined by the engineer's math skills.

CHAPTER 5

THE FUTURE

At present, there are roughly 200,000 robotics engineers in the United States. This is a large increase from the beginning of 2000. In the next 10 years, about 50,000 jobs are expected to be created.

The best locations for robotics engineering in the United States at present are the states along the East and West Coasts and in the Texas area. Alaska also offers a large number of jobs. The fewest positions are in the mid-northern states such as Nebraska, the Dakotas, Montana, and Wyoming.

One of the most attractive aspects of a robotics engineering career is the salary. Even at the entry level,

The robotics field has grown quickly since 2000 and is projected to see continued growth in the future.

The military uses robots to explore areas that are too dangerous for soldiers.

you can expect to make around $35,000 per year.
Experienced engineers can earn as much as $145,000 per
year, or even a bit more depending on the projects, the
company, and the location. The average nationwide salary
for a robotics engineer with a bachelor's degree is about
$50,000. Those who go on to earn their master's degree
receive a salary about 25 to 35 percent higher. The best-
paid positions tend to be with the federal government.
Private-sector positions are generally the next best paid,
followed by local government jobs and, lastly, state jobs.

There is little doubt that robots are going to become an important part of global society in the years ahead. Building materials are becoming less expensive, and robots for the consumer market are starting to gain ground. There are so many areas in which robots can still be introduced. A robot that checks the oil and tire pressure in a car? A robot that manages home-alarm systems? A robot that feeds the dog or cat every morning? Who knows what the next great robot will be—or who will design it? Maybe it will be you!

THINK ABOUT SCIENCE

Robotics engineering involves aspects of many other scientific disciplines—chemistry, physics, electronics, and computers. You will not merely be involved with a certain area of science, you'll be helping to develop it. It is one of the few fields where your individual and unique thinking will be put to good use virtually every day.

THINK ABOUT IT

After reading this book, what do you think makes a robotics engineer's job important?

Look online or visit a library to find out more about different types of robots. Try researching planetary rovers, surgical robots, geminoids, or driverless cars.

Reread chapters 2 and 3. How do robotics engineers use science and technology to perform their jobs?

LEARN MORE

FURTHER READING

Brown, Jordan, D. *Robo World: The Story of Robot Designer Cynthia Breazeal.* Washington, D.C.: Joseph Henry Press, 2006.

Furstinger, Nancy. *Helper Robots.* Minneapolis: Lerner, 2014.

Furstinger, Nancy. *Robots in Space.* Minneapolis: Lerner, 2014.

Manatt, Kathleen. *Robot Scientist.* Ann Arbor, MI: Cherry Lake, 2008.

Ventura, Marne. *Google Glass and Robotics Innovator Sebastian Thrun.* Minneapolis: Lerner, 2014.

WEB SITES

Kids Ahead—Robotics Cool Jobs
http://kidsahead.com/subjects/1-robotics/cool_jobs
Check out these exciting interviews with several successful robotics engineers.

PBS Kids—Tobey's Robot Workshop
http://pbskids.org/wordgirl/games/robotworkshop/
Play an animated game where you design your own robots.

Science Kids—Robots for Kids
www.sciencekids.co.nz/robots.html
Watch videos, take quizzes, and try a couple of cool experiments.

GLOSSARY

android (AN-droid) a robot designed to look like a human being

apprentice (uh-PREN-tis) a beginner who learns from an expert

automatons (AW-toh-muh-tahnz) machines that can move by themselves

hydraulics (hye-DRAW-liks) a branch of science that deals with the power created by liquid moving through pipes under pressure

intern (IN-turn) someone who works for very little or no money mainly to gain experience

microprocessing (mye-kroh-PRAH-ses-eng) the process of using a fully functional integrated computer circuit

prosthesis (pros-THEE-sis) a device that substitutes for a limb (or part of a limb) on the human body

prototype (PROH-tu-tipe) the first working model

simulation software (sim-yuh-LAY-shuhn SAWFT-wair) software designed to imitate a given set of circumstances or conditions

INDEX